GAINES: Who's (expletive deleted) idea was it to come out with this paperback?

WRITER #1: Well, sir, when we spoke to you yesterday, you said you'd jump off the nearest bridge before you'd run these stories.

GAINES: So?

WRITER #2: Well, after we heard you were fished out by the Coast Guard, we took that as a "go-ahead."

GAINES: You (expletive deleted)! Now we'll have to print the thing. Then they'll all know the (unclear) about what kind of (fuzzy) is inside Mad.

WRITER #3: Hey Chief, that's not a bad title for it . . . INSIDE MAD.

GAINES: And I suppose it'll have everything: MICKEY RODENT, SMILIN' MELVIN, BAT BOY AND RUBIN, SHERMLOCK SHOMES, PUZZLE PAGES and the rest of.

TOGETHER: Riiiiiight!

GAINES: And what will we charge for this (distorted . . . oooh, naughty-naughty).

TOGETHER: 95¢, of course!

GAINES: Nah! Do you know what I think of anyone who pays 95¢ for this . . . HMMMMMMMMMMM

(END OF REEL #1)

THE MAD READER

MAD STRIKES BACK!

and now...

CAW!
CAW! CAW!

ALBANY OR BUST

S.S. H.M.S. N.R.A.R.S.

BALLANTINE BOOKS • NEW YORK

William M. Gaines'

INSIDE
MAD

with a special Backword by
STAN FREBERG

Library of Congress Catalog Card Number: 55-12405

SBN 345-24427-3-095

First Printing: December, 1955
Twentieth Printing: April, 1975

First Canadian Printing: May, 1959
Third Canadian Printing: January, 1964

Printed in the United States of America

BALLANTINE BOOKS
A Division of Random House, Inc.
201 East 50th Street, New York, N.Y. 10022

CONTENTS

Foremost among the song parodists is a young Californian who has rocked the nation with such hits as "John and Marsha," "Try," and now "Rock and Roll Around Stephen Foster." You've seen his writing in Mad, Colliers *and other influential media. Now it gives us great pleasure to present this special Backword by Stan Freberg. Mr. Freberg . . .*

Well?

Where is he?

I don't see anybody.

Hold it. HOLD IT! You kids want to read Stan Freberg, don't you? Sure you do! Tell you what you do, then. Stan's Backword is around in the *back* of the book. Let's all turn to page 183 in our MAD books. Got that—page 183. Ready? Start turning!

INSIDE MAD

Animation Dept.: Here is a thought! Who amongst you have seen the sight of man turned beast? A hapless few, we trust! . . . And yet . . . though we are repelled at the sight of man turned beast . . . we revel to see beast turned man! When you pass along this thought . . . remember you saw it in MAD! . . . And now, our story . . .

MICKEY RODENT!

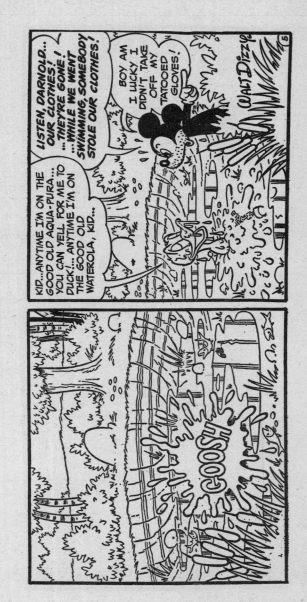

YOU THINK YOU CAN SHUT ME OUT WITH A GATE... WITHOUT MY CLOTHES?... I'LL GET BACK, BOY! I'LL GET BACK, SHVEINHUNT... I MEAN SHVEINMOUSE!

WE'LL SEE IF YOU GET BACK!... WE'LL SEE...

...FOR YEARS I'VE WATCHED YOU PUSHING YOUR WAY INTO MY ACT!... FOR YEARS I'VE WATCHED HOW YOU'VE COME!...YOU AND YOUR BLASTED RELATIVES... THEM THREE LITTLE NOONIK DUCKS!... I'VE SEEN YOU SLOWLY HUSTLING ME OUT OF THE PICTURE!... WELL I'M PUSHING YOU OUT, HERE AND NOW!

NOW I'VE GOT YOU WHERE I WANT YOU, DARNOLD DUCK! PEG-LEG POOP DIDN'T TAKE YOUR CLOTHES! I DID! IT WAS ALL PART OF MY PLAN TO GET YOU HERE!... FOR YEARS I'VE BEEN PLANNING THIS!

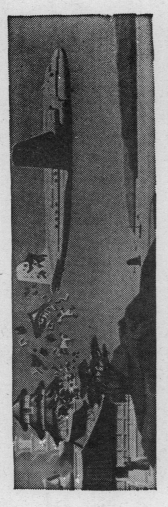

Canadian Specific

SPANS THE WORLD

For a world of service, travel Canadian Specific. Canadian Specific's 4-engined pressurized airliners fly from Canada to Hawaii, Fiji, New Zealand, Australia, Belgian Congo, Tibet, the North Pole, the Kremlin, the Moon and Kukamonga. By George! We take you anywhere! Canadian Specific's engined pressurized airliners have the straightest lines trailing out in back of the airplane drawings in their ads than any other airline.

I'M FLYIN' MY REAL LIFE-SIZE GAS ENGINE PLANE — YOU SEE THIS IS WHAT THAT LINE YOU ALWAYS SEE BEHIND THESE AIRPLANES IS THESE USED FOR.....

23

24

Science Dept.: You ever watch one of those sports newsreels where they've sped up the camera to slow down the action? By George, there's more going on than meets the eye! . . . Like forinstance, let us show you what happens to a ski jumper coming off the end of the jump . . . as seen by our camera in . . .

SLOW MOTION!

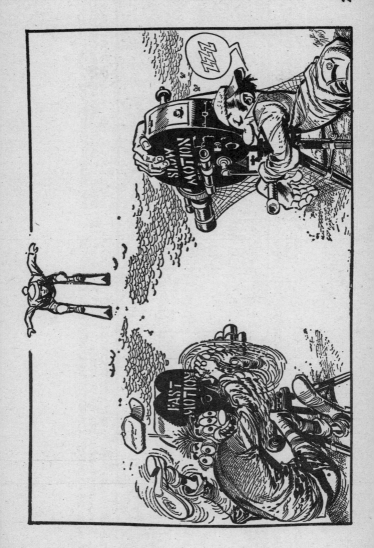

SKIERS ARE PROBABLY CRAZY, BUT WE'VE GOT SO USED TO WATCHING THEM THAT WE THINK NOTHING OF SEEING THE SKIER FLY THROUGH THE AIR AND FALL HUNDREDS OF FEET!

...WE THINK NOTHING OF SEEING HIM LAND IN A BIG FLURRY OF SNOW!... LITTLE DO YOU KNOW WHAT THINGS GO ON IN THAT BIG FLURRY OF SNOW!

THE FURSHLUGGINER SLOW-MOTION CAMERA HAS ALL THE ANSWERS!

...HERE, AFTER DESCENDING, OUR SKIER MAKES CONTACT WITH GROUND...

...THIS PARTICULAR SKIER HAS MADE VERY FAULTY LANDING!

...HERE, SKIER, BE-CAUSE OF FAULTY LAND-ING, LEAVES GROUND!

...HERE SKIER REACHES APEX OF FIRST BOUNCE AND IS READY TO DESCEND!!

THE FURSHLUGGINER SLOW-MOTION CAMERA HAS ALL THE ANSWERS!

...THIS PARTICULAR SKIER HAS MADE VERY FAULTY LANDING!

...HERE, AFTER DESCENDING, OUR SKIER MAKES CONTACT WITH GROUND...

...HERE, SKIER, BE-CAUSE OF FAULTY LAND-ING, LEAVES GROUND!

...HERE SKIER REACHES APEX OF FIRST BOUNCE AND IS READY TO DESCEND!

27

...HERE SKIER DESCENDS! ...NOTE SKIS COMPLETELY OUT OF LINE!

...HERE SKIER CONTACTS GROUND AGAIN. THIS TIME WITH BODY!

...NOTE HOW BODY FLATTENS FROM FORCE TO HALF ITS DEPTH!

...HERE SKIER BOUNCES UP FROM GROUND FOR THE SECOND TIME!

...NOTE REMARKABLE ELASTICITY AS SKIER RISES OUT OF CAMERA RANGE!

...NOTE FOR MOMENT WHILE SKIER IS OUT OF PICTURE, DEEP GOUGES IN SNOW!
...NOTE SKIER DESCENDS INTO PICTURE AGAIN, THIS TIME HEAD FIRST!
...NOTE HEAD ABOUT TO CONTACT GROUND WITH GREAT FORCE!
...NOTE FORCE WITH WHICH SNOW AND ROCKS ARE FLUNG FROM IMPACT!
...NOW NOTE SEPARATE PARTS OF SKIER AS THEY BOUNCE UP FOR LAST TIME!
5

TV Dept.: Our constant readers have no doubt noticed our sudden shift to television! We are giving special attention to TV because we believe it has become an integral part of living . . . a powerful influence in shaping the future . . . but mainly we are giving attention because we just got a new TV set!

So here's our story. . . .

HOWDY DOOIT!

37

NOW IN CASE YOUR MOTHER REFUSES TO BUY YOU A LOAF OF *SKWUSHY'S*, HERE'S WHAT TO DO! NOW MAKE BELIEVE I'M YOU AND MAKE BELIEVE THAT'S YOUR MOTHER SHOPPING IN THE SUPER-MARKET AND SHE DOESN'T WANT TO BUY BREAD TODAY!

...YOU JUST WAIT TILL HER BACK IS TURNED AND SLIP A LOAF OF SWUSHY'S INTO THE SHOPPING BASKET...HIDE IT WAY UNDER WHERE SHE CAN'T NOTICE IT!...THEN AGAIN...IF MOM HAPPENS TO BUY ANOTHER BRAND OF BREAD...

...WAIT TILL SHE GETS STUCK ON THE LINE AT THE CASHIER'S COUNTER AND QUICK SUBSTITUTE A LOAF OF *SKWUSHY'S!* SHE'LL HAVE TO BUY IT!.... BESIDES *SKWUSHY'S* WHITE BREAD, TRY *SKWUSHY'S* GREEN AND PURPLE BREAD!

41

45

PLEASE, BUFFALO BILL...DON'T BE JUVENILE!...IF ONE HAD THE CHOICE, IT WOULD PROBABLY BE SOUNDEST TO GET INTO A WHITE-COLLAR OCCUPATION SUCH AS AN INVESTMENT BROKER OR SOME - SUCH!

WELL...ON TO THE NEXT YOUNGSTER!...SONNY...WHAT WOULD YOU LIKE TO BE WHEN YOU GROW UP?...A POLICE CHIEF?...A FIREMAN? ...A INDIAN? OR, (HOT-DOG), MAYBE A JET-FIGHTER PILOT? HUH?

HUH? HUH? HUH?

...WHAT...MORE THAN ANYTHING ...ANYTHING ELSE ...WHAT...WHAT WOULD YOU LIKE TO DO DO!

KIN I LEAVE THE ROOM?

DOT PUZZLES

'DOT-PUZZLES,' GANG! LOTS OF KEEN FUN AHEAD FOR EVERYONE!

YOU MUST HAVE SEEN THIS FEATURE... HERE ARE TWO CONNECTING-DOT PUZZLES. THE FIRST ONE IS EASY... JUST A STARTER! IF YOU CAN COMPLETE IT, TRY YOUR HAND AT THE NEXT ONE WHICH IS SLIGHTLY MORE DIFFICULT! WHEN YOU GET ALL THE DOTS *CONNECTED,* THEY MAKE A *PICTURE!* GOSHAROOTIE! THEY CAN BE FRAMED N' EVERYTHING... WHY... *THEY TEACH YOU HOW TO DRAW!* SOME PUZZLE, HUH, GANG? *''* SOME FEATURE, HUH?

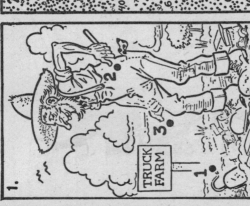

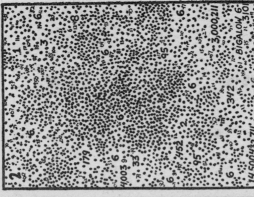

ANSWERS ON LAST PAGE!

Dollar for Dollar

You Can't Beat a

PUNTIAC

Famous For Dependability—The World Over!

When you drive a Puntiac Special cross-country, taking hills and mountains as they come . . . exploring little-known byways . . . covering the many miles a day the vast spaces of our big country require—that's when you most appreciate Puntiac Special's big-car performance.

You're easy and relaxed behind that mighty power plant—the most thoroughly proved engine in any car. Police cars are no problem—your Puntiac Special is so nimble and alert. You ride without annoying bullets going past your head. The thick, bullet proof glass takes care of that. You step on the accelerator and pull away from that police car as if it were going in reverse, for Puntiac Special provides the quick-start and pick-up that bank robbers so often need in a pinch.

Sounds good? You'll like this even better when you've covered the many miles a day you require to make your getaway. Puntiac Special is specially priced for bank robbers. And why not. You'll have to rob a bank to pay the price. See your Puntiac dealer today.

PUNTIAC DIVISION OF GENERAL MURDERS INCORPORATED

Puntiac Special's trunk space is phenomenal You can store away a whole arsenal besides a human body. And there'll be plenty of room to spare for your extra suitcases of money.

This is the story of the men who go alone into the Wild Blue Yonder . . . the unsung heroes who go fearlessly, not for riches, not for glory . . . into the Wild Blue Yonder . . . some never to return! Ah yes . . . the Wild Blue Yonder Bar and Grill, where we find the hero of our story . . .

SMILIN' MELVIN!

62

THAT KAPPOKKITTA-ING... GETTING LOUDER, LOUDER! IT'S NO USE! I'VE GOTTA HIT THE SEAT EJECTOR BUTTON! I'VE *GOTTA BAIL OUT!*

THAT KAPPOKKITTA-POKKITTA, SOUND IN THE ENGINE!... I DON'T LIKE IT... SHOULD I STAY WITH THE SHIP AND TRY TO SAVE 'ER OR SHOULD I DITCH 'ER!

LISTEN TO THAT MOTOR... PURRING LIKE A SEWING MACHINE... *A SEWING MACHINE???* THIS IS AN AIRPLANE... *NOT A SEWING MACHINE!*

64

AIR MEET TUES.
SPACE MEET SAT.
THAT WAS JOE TOWER... BEST RADIOMAN IN TOWN! WHAT AN OPERATOR!
TAKE 'ER UP AS FAR AS SHE'LL GO, SMILIN' MELVIN! ...CLIMB! CLIMB!
...CLIMB AS HIGH AS YOU CAN GO, BWAH!
?
POST NO BILLS
UGH! IF ONLY I HAD A LADDER ALONG, I COULD CLIMB A LITTLE HIGHER! IF I HAD EVEN A FOOT-STOOL!
AIR MEET TODAY AUNT JENNY'S TEA ROOM – FLYING SAUCERS
5

...IT WAS THE SECRET-SUPER-TURBO-HYPER-PTOOEY-JET X-13! YOU GOT INTO THE **WRONG PLANE** BY MISTAKE! YOU GOT INTO A PLANE THAT WAS TESTED AND FLOWN **MONTHS AGO!**

BUT BEFORE I DO, THERE IS SOMETHING I MUST TELL YOU! THAT PLANE YOU JUST TESTED... THE SECRET-SUPER-TURBO-HYPER-PTOOEY JET X-13?... WELL... IT WASN'T THE SECRET-SUPER-TURBO-HYPER PTOOEY-JET **X-13...**

YOU ARE SO BRAVE AND I HAVE BEEN SO MEAN TO YOU, SMILIN' MELVIN! I AM GOING TO REPENT! I AM GOING TO DO SOMETHING TO MAKE UP FOR ALL MY SINS.... AND THAT IS.... TO SHOW YOU THE **SECRET ATTRACTION I HAVE IN MY FACE!**

You who love the sound of the sighing forest . . . you who love the sight of the sparkling mountain lake . . . you who love the feel of the squooshing cow pasture . . . you who hoo you hoohoo you! His name was his trade mark . . . his trade mark his name . . . and that's his name . . .

CLIK CLINK CLAK SNAP CLAK CLUK
CLIK CLIK GLIKSY
CLIK CLIK
CLAC CLEK CLIK BID SNIP
CLAK CLIKETTY SNIP
SNAP CLIK
SNAP SNAP CLOOK

...STEADY, MEN... DON'T SHOOT YET... WAIT TILL IT GETS CLOSER BEFORE YOU SHOOT... STEADY,... STEADY,...

SHOOT!

WAIT! LOOK!.. IT'S TURNING AROUND!.IT'S LOOKING AT US! ...IT'S GETTING READY TO CHARGE!.. TAKING OUT ITS CREDIT CARD GETTING READY TO CHARGE!

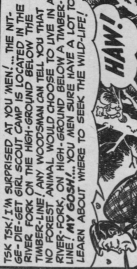

AHA, MEN!... LOOK!... A RARE FIND!... YOU ARE IN FOR A VERY SPECIAL TREAT... A SIGHT THAT WILL THRILL YOU FOR WE HAVE COME UPON SOMETHING UP AHEAD THAT YOU WILL NEVER FORGET!
CAMP NIT-GE-DIE-GET?
...WE HAVE COME UPON A RARE AMERICAN BEAVER AT WORK... A FANTASTIC ANIMAL WHO CUTS DOWN THE TREES... TRIMS THE BRANCHES... A TRULY BREATH-TAKING SIGHT!
CAMP NIT-GE-DIE-GET?
...THEN DRAGS THE BRANCHES TO THE WATER... SETS THEM UP... BUILDS A STRUCTURE... CONSTRUCTS ROOMS INSIDE... WITH RUNNING WATER... WITH VENTILATION... WITH RENT PRICE-FIXED?!... YOU WILL NEVER FORGET THIS SIGHT!
CAMP NIT-GE-DIE-GET?
2

83

...BY GEORGE, COME TO THINK OF IT, THAT IS A LOT OF MONEY!

DID THEY THINK I WOULD KILL YOU FOR $5,000?

DOWN-WIND, BOY!

DID THEY THINK THAT I WOULD KILL YOU FOR A MAGAZINE COVER, SANDY? DID THEY THINK I WOULD KILL YOU FOR MONEY?

SANDY?...HUNT KILL AND BRING BACK DEAD YOU, SANDY? DID THEY THINK I WOULD DO THIS TO YOU?

WHEN I WAS OUT WITH NATURE, I FROZE IN THE WINTER... I BOILED IN THE SUMMER... AND EVERYWHERE I WENT... BUGS, BUGS, BUGS, BUGS, BUGS! I HATE NATURE! I HATE IT! I HATE IT! I HATE IT!

...A GERM-RIDDEN NATURAL FLY THAT GOT IN HERE WHEN I OPENED THE DOOR FOR YOU!... YOU KNOW HOW MANY PEOPLE DIE FROM FLIES?... YOU KNOW HOW MANY PEOPLE DIE FROM NATURE?

CRASH

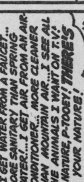

...I GET WATER FROM A FAUCET... MORE SANITARY THAN SPRING WATER!... I GET AIR FROM AN AIR-CONDITIONER... MORE CLEANER THAN MOUNTAIN AIR... I SEE ALL THE ANIMALS I WANT ON T.V.! ...NATURE, P-TOOEY! THERE'S YOUR NATURE!

THE MAZE *

...YOU ARE CHASING A MAIDEN WHO HAS BEEN KIDNAPPED BY A GIANT...FOR YOU ARE A KNIGHT!... CAN YOU FIND THE RIGHT ROAD THAT THE GIANT HAS TAKEN?

ANSWERS ON LAST PAGE!

*—NO RELATION TO WILLIE!

Cinema Dept.: You know how sometimes movie ads give a phony impression?!... like forinstance... take a scene from a typical...

Advertising Dept.: ... So then the Hollywood ad men get ahold of the scene, and here's what you see in the newspapers ...

...GET THE GENERAL IDEA?... LIKE FOR INSTANCE...A WAR PICTURE BEGINS... G.I.'S SLOGGING THROUGH THE MUD!

...FOR TEN REELS THEY GO, ALL SHMEARED WITH DIRT AND BEARDS... SLOGGING THROUGH THE MUD!

FINALLY THEY REACH THE ACTION! *BLAM*— *BLAM!* A ENEMY SOLDIER FALLS OFF A CLIFF! THE GOOD GUYS WIN THE HILL!

...AND THAT'S THE WAY THE PICTURE ENDS WITH THE G.I.'S SLOGGING OFF THROUGH THE MUD...

...SO AFTER SEEING ONE GIRL FOR ONLY TWO SECONDS IN A TWO HOUR PICTURE... HERE'S THE WAY THE ADVERTISEMENT GOES...

AND THEN THE LIEUTENANT ORDERS THE MEN OUT BECAUSE THERE'S ALWAYS ANOTHER HILL TO CONQUER!

THE VICTORIOUS G.I.'S MARCH INTO THE LIBERATED TOWN!...FOR TWO SECONDS, A GIRL JUMPS OUT AND KISSES A SOLDIER!

WAR HELL WAR

THE STORY OF SOLDIERS AND THE WOMEN THEY LOVED!

Starring ROARY LYON AND VAVA VOOM

AND A THOUSANDS OF CASTS

in SCATHING CYNICOLOR

Pakpants PRESENTS

...FINALLY... AN ADVENTURE PICTURE!... THIS GIRL IS SICK SOMEWHERE IN BROOKLYN, SEE? SHE'S NAUSEOUS!

SHE HAS A RARE INCURABLE DISEASE SO SHE GOES TO MIAMI! A PILOT STRUCK BY HER BEAUTY... FALLS...

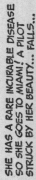

...OFF THE WING OF HIS PLANE! IT REALLY ISN'T HIS PLANE AND WHEN HE FLIES TO KUKAMONGA, THE REAL OWNER HITS HIM...

...BECAUSE HE'S SUCH A SLOPPY PILOT! ANYHOW...THE PILOT MEETS THE GIRL AGAIN IN BANFF, AT THE AQUARIUM...

SHE FLEES ON A BOAT TO POONA WHERE HE CATCHES HER AND AS SHE LEANS NAUSEOUS OVER THE RAIL...

...SHE TELLS HIM OF HER INCURABLE DISEASE! HE MARRIES HER ANYHOW./THEY GO TO SEE VESUVIUS ON THEIR HONEYMOON!

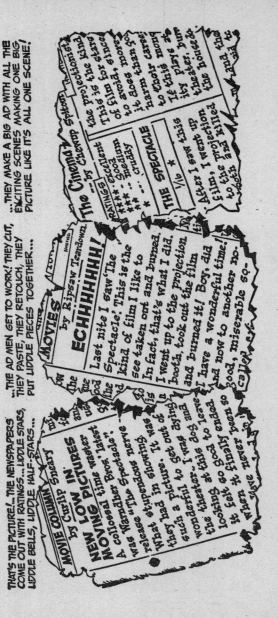

THAT'S THE PICTURE!... THE NEWSPAPERS COME OUT WITH RATINGS... LIDDLE STARS, LIDDLE BELLS, LIDDLE HALF-STARS...

...THE AD MEN GET TO WORK! THEY CUT, THEY PASTE, THEY RETOUCH, THEY PUT LIDDLE PIECES TOGETHER...

...THEY MAKE A BIG AD WITH ALL THE EXCITING SCENES MAKING ONE BIG PICTURE LIKE IT'S ALL ONE SCENE!

MOVIE COLUMN
by Curlyp Sneary

NEW IN LOW PICTURES

MOVING time waeter latest

A colossal Warndher Bros.' latest
release "The Spectacle".
What had in showing. It was
they had in a picture. It was
such a picture. I was dying
wonderful. I was and
the theater at this dog to leave
looking at this dog ended so
it felt so good ended so
when it finally been so
have never been in...

MOVIES
by Ripsaw Teardown.

ECHHHHHHH!

Last nite I saw The
Spectacle! This is the
kind of film I like to
see taken out and burned.
In fact, that's what I did.
I went up to the projection
booth, took out the film
and burned it! Boy, did
I have a wonderful time!
And now to another so-
good, miserable so-
called...

The Cinema
--by Chewup Spitem

the projectionst
This is for the stars
of film, since
to avoid, however,
it does more
harm than care!
to their mon
If this plays at
ivy plays, burn
ivy theater,
the house d...

RATINGS
**** -- excellent
*** -- good
** -- fair
* -- cruddy

THE SPECTACLE

1/10 *

After I saw this
film, I went up
to the projection
booth, and killed
the 2nd and the
and th...

...THOUSANDS OF MILES APART, THE SCENES ARE TAKING PLACE...SO THEY MAKE IT ONE SCENE...LIKE THIS...

...THOUSANDS OF MILES APART, THE SCENES ARE TAKING PLACE...SO THEY MAKE IT ONE SCENE...LIKE THIS...

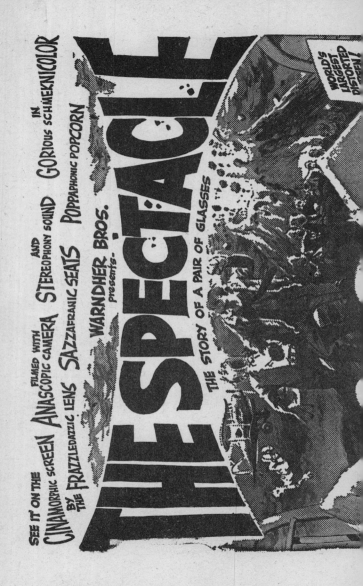

THIS SCENE WILL STEAM YOUR GLASSES

Starring - VAVA VOW - Have you met Vava Vow ....the 3-D ; WHAM ; girl ?

Produced by - HERMAN LENTH   Directed by - MOE BREDTH   Written by MELVIN DEPFTH

Says Movie Columnist
CURLIP SNEARY -

"New ... A colossal time ...
...stupendous... wonderful ...
ties of good "'"

Says critic
RIPSAW TEARDOWN -

" This is the kind of film I
like to see... Boy, did I
have a wonderful time..."

Says writer
CHEWUP SPITOUT -
... "for stars'"...

(★ ★ ★
★ ★)

Newspaper Cartoon Dept.: Today we present two charming boys who for years have been making mischief on such a scale that although it isn't publicized, they have made their home a shambles and laid waste to the land!... Yes... You guessed it!...Those two lovable little rascals, Hans and Feetz...The...

KATCHANDHAMMER KIDS!

123

132

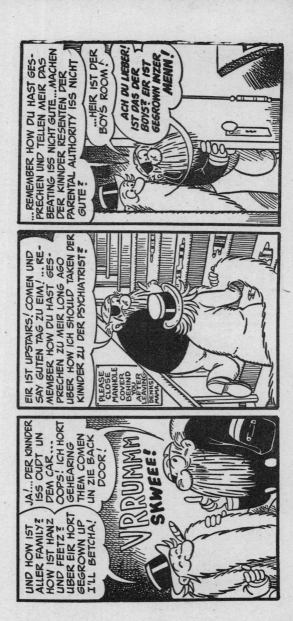

"PLAYING CROQUET ON THE FRONT LAWN," by Bill Elder, Number 1 in the series "Booze Life in America."

Beer and ale—mealtime favorites

In this friendly, freedom-loving land of ours—*beer belongs...enjoy it!*

AMERICA'S BEVERAGE OF MODERATION

Sponsored by the Brewer's Foundation to Encourage Excess

Hero Worship Dept.: You have heard of those two masked batlike crime fighters of Gotham City.... You have heard of their exciting deeds, of their constant war against the underworld!... This story, then... This story, then... has *absolutely nothing* to do with them! This story is about two different people....

144

147

150

Panel 1: PUT AWAY YOUR VIALS, YOUR WEAPONS, YOUR MECHANICAL DEVICES! THIS SITUATION CALLS FOR HAND-TO-HAND COMBAT!... MAINLY *WRASSLING!*

RIGHT!

Panel 2: LOOK! THE FLURGLE GANG IS MADE UP OF WOMEN!... QUICK LEMME AT MY GAS VIALS!

GAS VIALS! YOU WOULDN'T USE GAS VIALS ON WOMEN WOULD YOU, BAT BOY?

HANDS OFF, YOU DUMKOPF... I'M LOOKING FOR MY SECRET VIAL OF 'ARRID' SPRAY DEODORANT!

WELL-P... THAT TAKES CARE OF THE FLURGLE GANG!... THERE ARE NO MORE GANGS LEFT IN COSMOPOLIS! THERE WILL BE NO MORE MURDERS! LETS HOP ONTO OUR BAT-O-CYCLES AND PEDAL HOME TO HEADQUARTERS!

PHEW! WHAT A DAY! SOMETIMES I WONDER, SINCE YOU ARE A WEALTHY YOUNG SOCIALITE IN REAL LIFE, WHY YOU KEEP KNOCKING YOURSELF OUT ON THIS 'BAT BOY' KICK! IT DON'T PAY, YOU KNOW!
RUBIN! THERE ARE OTHER THINGS IN LIFE BESIDES MONEY... FINER THINGS! ...THINGS THAT CANNOT BE BOUGHT... THINGS MUCH BETTER! FINER THAN MONEY!... THINGS LIKE... LIKE... LIKE POWER! RRROW! WURF! GRRR!
...NOW HANG UP MY CAPE LIKE A GOOD FELLOW!
HQ

WHAT'S WRONG WITH THIS PICTURE?

HAVING FUN, GANG?... BET YOU ARE...MAINLY SINCE THIS IS THE LAST NAUSEATING PAGE IN THIS PUZZLE-PAGE FIASCO! IN THE FOLLOWING PICTURES, THE ARTIST HAS MADE A NUMBER OF MISTAKES! SEE IF YOU CAN FIND AND LIST THEM...NEEDLESS TO SAY, THE ARTIST WILL BE FIRED AS PROMPTLY AS POSSIBLE SINCE THIS COMPANY DOES VERY GOOD HIGH-CLASS ART WORK USING ONLY THE BEST AND WE KICK OUT ALL ARTISTS WHO MAKE MISTAKES!

WHAT'S WRONG WITH THIS PICTURE?

ANSWERS ON LAST PAGE!

157

A fog lies thick on London, giving a lonely, eerie quality to the night sounds! . . . The ominous chiming of Big Ben . . . the footsteps of *something* scuttling by . . . the hollow clack of Dr. Whatsit's head coming in contact with a lamppost as he rushes through the fog to see his old friend . . .

SHERMLOCK SHOMES!

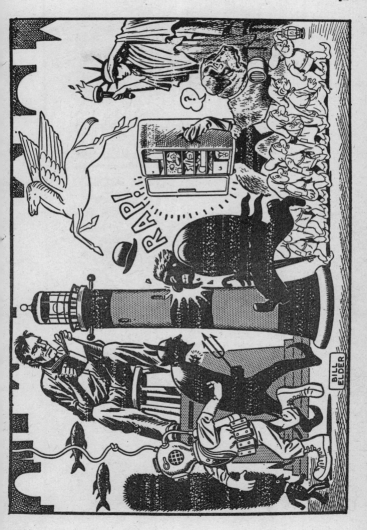

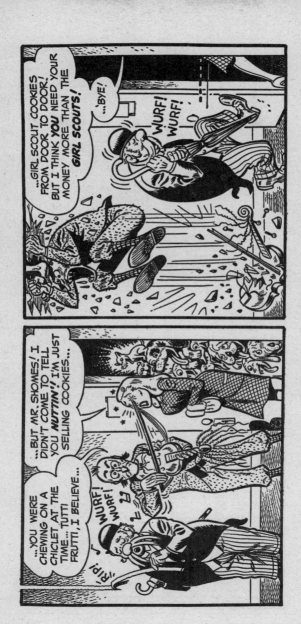

169

4

177

IF YOU NOTICE, THE MANTLEPIECE COMES LOOSE! AS THE MURDERED MAN STUDIED THE DOOR KNOB, GETTING HIS FINGERPRINTS ALL OVER IT, THE MURDERER STEPPED OUT....

IMAGINE THE MURDERED MAN'S SURPRISE WHEN HE TRIED TO STUFF THE DOOR KNOB INTO HIS PIPE! THIS WAS THE MOMENT THE MURDERER HAD BEEN WAITING FOR!

THE MURDERER THEN VERY CLEVERLY SLIPPED A DUPLICATE DOOR-KNOB MECHANISM INTO THE MURDERED MAN'S JAR OF SHAG-TOBACCO!

THE WAY I WAS KILLED... AFTER LOCKING MYSELF IN MY STUDY, I TRIPPED AND FELL AGAINST THE MANTLEPIECE... SMASH-ING MY HEAD IN! IT WAS AN ACCIDENT!

SHOMES! SCOTLAND YARD ARRESTS YOU FOR THE MURDER OF DR. WHATSIT! WE WARN YOU...ANYTHING YOU SAY WILL BE HELD AGAINST YOU!

MARILYN MONROE! ...LANA TURNER! ...HEDY LAMARR! ...*!?!*

...AND THAT MURDERER IS YOU, MADAM... ARTY-MORTY IN DISGUISE!... CAH-MON, ARTY... TAKE OFF THAT WIG! SCOTLAND YARD IS ON THE WAY! YOU MIGHT AS WELL CONFESS!

HEY! ...HE'S ...CRAZY!!

ANSWER PAGE
BILL ELDER DREWD THEM

DOT PICTURES

1.

2.

THE MAZE

PRETTY TOUGH PUZZLE, EH GANG?
BUT THAT'S BECAUSE YOU DIDN'T
FOLLOW THE DIRECTIONS...BECAUSE
YOU WEREN'T SHARP-WITTED...
BECAUSE YOU DIDN'T GO 'ROUND
THE OUTSIDE AND COME IN
OVER HERE...

BEGIN

FINISH

WHAT'S WRONG WITH THIS PICTURE?

BETTER STILL YOU SHOULD ASK...WHAT'S *RIGHT*
WITH THIS PICTURE!!

BACKWORD BY STAN FREBERG

That fortunate legion of us tuned in on the MAD wave length, and therefore receptive to the mighty impulses radiating from its Furshlugginer-active[1] pages, will immediately recognize the wisdom of a Backword. I feel, therefore, that no explanation is necessary. True, a few preoccupied shoppers may whisk the book home thinking it is Norman Vincent Peale or at least "The Mollie Goldberg Cookbook." No matter. These people, being too pseudo-blasé or just plain dull to receive the MAD radiations, will (a) suffer an intense migraine headache four pages in, and (b) fling the book out the window.

So that takes care of *them*.

This leaves a number of non-MAD-addicts who, because of their superior intelligence, will (a) see instantly the brilliant lampoonery that is MAD, (b) curse themselves soundly for having been behind the door when MAD was handed out, and (c) howl all the way through. By the time they will have reached the Backword, their brain-pans will have been conditioned to accept such things without a question. They will have become "MADDICTS" and therefore one of us. And *we* don't need any explanation of a Backword, do we? So the sooner you get it through your potrzebie that there won't be any explanation the better—and that's final now! Crimenentles!

Where was I? Oh, yes, the Backword. For the uninformed, MAD started out three years ago as a comic book kidding only other comic strips. It has graduated today into a first-rate humor magazine, kidding not only comic strips but movies, TV, novels, commercial ads or anything it feels like. Merely to say that I am a fan of this magazine would be like saying that Gina Lollo-

[1] Similar to "radio-active" but with fewer commercials.

brigida is "sort of interesting." I am addicted to MAD like the Aga Khan to starches. Why? Because it makes me laugh, and I am rather fond of laughing.

Fortunately, MAD loves to laugh at the same things I do—that is to say, we are both completely insane. MAD does the same thing in a literary (or illiterary) form that I try to do on phonograph records, which is to point up some of the absurdities of mankind through the medium of satire. In a world where things get a shade ridiculous at times, satire is a very important thing to mental health. It lets a little of the air out of people and things who take themselves too seriously and deserve to be brought back down to earth. It also gives everyone a good healthy laugh into the bargain.

MAD is an example of pure and honest satire, written brilliantly by my friend Harvey Kurtzman, and drawn hysterically by Jack Davis, Bill Elder and Wallace Wood. I cannot praise their combined efforts enough. This volume, for example, is taken from several issues of the original MAD and is all written by Harvey. My favorite is "Smilin' Melvin." You may like "Superduperman."[2]

In closing, let us remember that someone once said "Laughter is the best medicine." It is a true fact that a friend of mine had an acquaintance who fell into poor health and proceeded to decline a little each day until the doctors could do nothing for him. Upon being told that the patient was beyond medical help, my friend called one day at his bedside and on a hunch told him a very funny joke he had just heard regarding three wild animals and a man who played the violin.[3] As he reached the punch line, the pale man opened his eyes and laughed for the first time in months. Color returned to his face, and would you believe it?—within forty-eight hours . . . he was dead. The laughter had overtaxed him. This shows how much the guy knew who said "Laughter is the best medicine." HOO HAH!

It is possible, of course, that he meant "Laughter is the best *tasting* medicine." This really shows you what a nudnick he was! I know of some much more daring medicines. I know of a

[2] You may like it but you won't get it, it's in another collection. What do you expect for 35¢ anyway?

[3] This joke is available on request.

cough sirup, for example, that tastes just like Manischewitz Wine when you pour it over the rocks. (It doesn't taste bad over ice, either.) Make this simple test at home: Pour first the cough sirup into a tall glass, then the laughter. See how much of a belt you get out of the laughter! I rest my case.

It seems pointless to go on because I think I have covered the subject adequately, and also because we are running out of paper. Those wishing to read the conclusion of my Backword will find it (with a fine magnifying glass) on the edge of this page in Sanskrit. The body of my message has been put across by now anyhow, which is simply that MAD is my favorite pastime (next to girls) and I hope you have enjoyed INSIDE MAD as much as I did. I boiled mine for dinner.

STAN FREBERG

WOWEE GANG!
THE GOLDEN AGE
OF MAD IS HERE AGAIN!

THE MAD READER with a Vital Message from Roger Price—
Superduperman! — Newspapers! — Starchie — Flesh Garden! —
Dragged Net!—The Face on the Floor!—Meet Miss Potgold—
Gasoline Valley!—Lone Stranger!   95¢

MAD STRIKES BACK! with a Straight Talk by Bob & Ray—Prince
Violent!—Captain Tvideo!—Gopo Gossum!—Ping Pong!—Poop-
eye!—Teddy and the Pirates!—Believe It or Don't—Cowboy!—
Manduck and the Magician.   95¢

INSIDE MAD with a Backword by Stan Freberg—Mickey Rodent!
—Slow Motion—Howdy Dooit!—Puzzle Pages—Smilin' Melvin!
—Mark Trade!—Movie . . . Ads—Katchandhammer Kids!—Bat
Boy and Rubin!—Shermlock Shomes!   95¢

UTTERLY MAD—Melvin of the Apes!—Book! Movie!—Robin
Hood!—G. I. Shmoe!—Frank N. Stein!—Little Orphan Melvin!—
The Raven!   95¢

THE BROTHERS MAD—Black and Blue Hawks!—Newspaper Col-
umns—Woman Wonder—How to Get into the Army—Shadow—
Hound of the Basketballs—The Dave Garrowunway Show—Con-
fidentially . . . plus cast of thousands.   95¢ cheap

To order by mail, send price of book(s) plus
50¢ per order for handling to Ballantine Cash
Sales, P.O. Box 505, Westminster, Maryland
21157. Please allow three weeks for delivery.